On a
Grey Thread

On a Grey Thread

Elsa Gidlow

MINT EDITIONS

On a Grey Thread was first published in 1923.

This edition published by Mint Editions 2021.

ISBN 9781513283456 | E-ISBN 9781513288475

Published by Mint Editions®

 MINT
EDITIONS

minteditionbooks.com

Publishing Director: Jennifer Newens
Design & Production: Rachel Lopez Metzger
Project Manager: Micaela Clark
Typesetting: Westchester Publishing Services

To
You Few
For Whom These Were Written and You Many
Who May Read

Contents

EPILOGUE 81

THE GREY THREAD

THE GREY THREAD

My life is a grey thread,
A thin grey stretched out thread,
And when I trace its course, I moan:
How dull! How dead!

But I have gay beads.
A pale one to begin,
A blue one for my painted dreams,
And one for sin,
Gold with coiled marks,
Like a snake's skin.

For love an odd bead
With a deep purple glow;
A green bead for a secret thing
That few shall know;
And yellow for my thoughts
That melt like snow.

A red bead for my strength,
And crimson for my hate;
Silver for the songs I sing
When I am desolate;
And white for my laughter
That mocks dull fate.

My life is a grey thread
Stretching through Time's day;
But I have slipped gay beads on it
To hide the grey.

YOUTH

YOUTH

I must go down,
Down, down,
Below the crusts of things,
Under the shadows,
Into thought-haunted places
Where few go;
Where the road is broken
And travelled by monsters,
Truths with hard sphinx-faces.

I must go down
Into the caves of life,
Into the darknesses,
Deep, deep,
Below the good of things,
Below the evil of things,
Where the calm roots of wisdom creep.

I must tunnel
Under the bloom of dreams,
Under the frame-work of fancies,
Tunnel alone.
What if I shatter frail things,
Break delicate flowers of myth
Timorous dreamers have sown?

I must go down
Below narrow roads men have made,
Below bridging lies men have built,
Into the caverns of truth.
I know pain is waiting there
Eager to break me,
But I am strong.
I have faith in my youth.

Living is crusted with lies.
I want life naked,
Laughing and young.
Not fettered, not tamed,
But life unashamed,
With the cry of Desire on her tongue.

WORLD CRY

There are gods in the market place.
Did you know there were gods there?
All, yes. Gods, gods,
There are gods everywhere.
I think the many like gods,
I think they like to pray and mourn.
For a joy-song their prophets sing:
"A new God will soon be born!"
For a joy-song I would sing:
"Let every god be down-torn."
But what is the world muttering?
Has she whispered it since life began?
"Gods! I want none of your gods.
Look to yourself—Man."

HOPE

You would win me, woo me, win me,
To be your lover, Hope!
You would lure me, charm me, lure me,
With all your deathless youth!
You would have me worship, adore you,
Build my life for you;
Mould my moments into hours
Out of your careless smile!
How you pursue me, woo me, follow,
Like a light-headed girl.
All the world is your willing lover:
What do you want with me?

You are a wanton, lovely, perfect,
A dazzling thing like day,
Draped with silk things,
Tasselled, jewelled,
Hung about with veils;
Painted with sweet lies men have blended
Of folly and dreams and fear.
You are a wanton, all men's mistress:
What do you want with me?
What are your gifts worth, light bestower?
All lips know your kiss.

What is your word worth, soft-tongued liar?
You have deceived all men.
Why do you follow, woo me, follow,
Like a light-headed girl?
What can I give you? What can you give me?
What do you want with me?
Painted wanton! Tasselled Houri!
Gay in your dress of shame!
You are all men's willing mistress.
What do *I* want with you?

Life's Leaders

Their clouded wine, their whited bread,
We cannot take and call it good;
Yet sorrier fare Life grudges us
Who have no taste for common food.

We must go hungry long life through,
Aching and hungry to the end;
Betrayed by pity into chains
Reason tries vainly to transcend.

Are we not sadly prodigal?
We spend ourselves without restraint;
Yea, we let Beauty break our hearts
And bleed for love until we faint.

Yet it is not the thorns, the shame,
Not the hurt body's weak distress:
Our bitterest crucifixion lies
In man's abject unworthiness.

From Life's rough cloth and flying threads,
From dust, from passion, dreams and pain,
From the dear madness men call love,
From faith that lies beyond the brain,

We shape the only deathless soul
That mortal man will ever know.
Behold his gratitude, these stones.
They say't is by the heart we grow.

Still we build quietly and wait.
The heart may break; the heart is frail;
But a stern, strange ecstasy
Befriends us; and we dare not fail.

The Hand that points the solemn way
May be a wanton hand at best;
The great Word echoing in our souls
May be a bored God's casual jest.

We cannot guess. We only know
'T is written by some awful Pen
We must be torches sacrificed
To light the way for lesser men.

MARKET MAZE

Faces, faces. . .
Restless faces and restless hands,
Not the divine restlessness
Of seeking, singing spirits.
Not the impatient restlessness
Of a creature mad for wings.
But a feeble thing,
A futile thing:
The restlessness of the market place,
The fever of buying and selling.

GRAIN AND GRAPES

GRAIN AND GRAPES

This word came to me
From one whose wisdom shapes
The destiny of many:
Let your thought be fruitful:
Men like grain and grapes.

I'll not be loved of men for my gifts
If men want grain and grapes alone:
My thoughts are gnarled, fantastic trees,
Grown up untended, barely pruned,
From ancient seed I have not sown.

Their snake-mouthed roots are in my heart.
I feel them hungrily intense
Drawing the seething love-sap out.
Prodigally I feed them all
My being's vivid afluence.

But thus far they have only borne
Veined blue buds that bloom to be
Scarred flowers of inhuman pain,
And little opening leaves, like eyes
Full of a grave futility.

Strange flowers foretell strange fruit
And gods stay breathless while they grow.
Men call and look for grain and grapes,
Their homely, humble earth-warm fruits;
But heaven is silent. The gods may know.

Oversoul

My laughter rings in the highest mountains,
My mockery echoes vividly over the peaks,
My laughter and my mockery dance lightly together
Like derisive imps. . . But my soul never speaks.
My wisdom sits on a promontory
And remotely overwatches the world;
My pain stays forever in that cave
Where the ragged ends of life come unfurled.
My love cuts downward between mountains
Like a torrential cataract, to the deeps,
For love, like life, is a down-going.
But my soul is like a thing that sleeps.
It knows the remorseless depths,
The thinnest ether of the farthest height;
There are no lights or darknesses for its discovering,
It has crawled on the earth and it knows the joy of flight.
It is speechless because it knows all speeches,
Future and present and what has gone before.
It waits sphinxlike, and I myself
Cannot guess what it is waiting for.

Come And Lie With Me

Come and lie with me and love me,
Bitterness.
Touch me with your hands a little,
Kiss me, as you lean above me,
With your cold sadistic kisses;
Wind your hair close, close around me,
Pain might dissipate this blankness.
Hurt me even, even wound me,
I have need of love that stings.
Come and lie with me and love me,
Bitterness,
So that I may laugh at things.

FUTILITY

Under all beauty that I know,
All vital dreams,
Sharp loveliness,
Under the hair, the lips of laughter,
The dusk-dim eyes of pain,
Lurks the single thing I fear,
Hard-mouthed, implacable-eyed,
The monster,
The satyr-thing, futility.

I cannot look on loveliness
Or burn the flame of ecstasy,
Or even dream for very long,
Without the annihilating fear
That it will suddenly tear some veil
And bare its dreadful face.

When I am light with the exaltation
Mysteriously born of worship,
Filled like a cup with the wine of wonder
At some great cloudy bloom of color,
Or learning the infinite secrets of rapture
With bared heart held to love's lips—
Light's eyes are suddenly blinded,
Life gropes in empty twilight,
And the mocking mouth of the satyr-thing
Leers at me from a veil of dust.

Shuddering I crouch to earth,
Trembling lest it come more near,
Trembling lest it stretch a hand
And touch me! Choked by an agony
Of horror lest its deadly eyes
Should shrivel my flaming heart of dream.
Sometimes I think the universe,
Mind, passion, beauty, wisdom, light,

All fathomless life-wonders,
Serve only for its cloak.

It lurks like death in everything
That has a singing heart:
In all exultant voices,
In all desire's burning eyes,
In youth's true soul,
In love's slim hands.

Sometimes I think it is life's core,
This mocking-mouth'd implacable ghost.
Sometimes I think it is life's core.
Sometimes I think it must be God.

Roots

O heavily weighing earth! O grim travail
In sunless silence with no hope of light!
O impotent wine! O bracken-food of pain!
I accept you all. I accept the timeless blight
Of crawling like a worm with unclean things,
Of being forever a yearning voiceless root
Bedded in this unwarmed oblivion
So that the great sun mellow my ultimate fruit.

I Must Be Far

I must be far from men and women
To love their ways.
I must be on a mountain
Breathing greatly like a tree
If my heart would yearn a little
For the peopled, placid valley.
I must be in a bare place
And lonely as a moon
To find the graceless ways of people
Worthful as a flower's ways,
A flower that lives for loveliness
And dies when beauty dies.

I cannot find music
On the tongues of men and women
Unless I hear their voices
Like echoes, silence-softened.
Their many words mean little.
Their mouths are blatant sparrows.

I must be far from men and women,
As God is far away,
To keep my faith with Beauty,
My heart sweet towards them,
And love them with a god's tranquility.

ECSTASY

Stars, turn from your courses,
Stars, stars, I want you,
Spill into my hands.
I have found a new loneliness,
A new strong loneliness,
That no one understands.

I know a new joy, stars,
A joy of the still peak,
The wonder of airs knife-sharp;
Stars, I have learned to know them,
I have learned the tongue they speak.
Stars, I can understand them,
All the words they say,
All the subtle things.
They teach me exaltation,
A new intoxication
Fine drawn as the music of harp-strings.
Alone. . . alone. . . alone. . .
Stars, I can hear my skin breathe,
Hear my blood beat.
How can flesh be so light,
Feet walk and touch nothing,
Thought become so fleet?

Time is a rhymeless poem
Without any end
Written in space,
Here at the world's summit
Where life-giving winds
Sharply whip one's face.
Life is the one reality,
Life intensely realized,
Life wildly felt;
Death is an ungrasped dream,
A vague monstrous fable,

A puzzle still unspelt.
Alone. . . alone. . . alone. . .

No other thing that breathes
In this keen place.
O my new joy,
Joy of singing summits,
Of endless, vibrant space!
Stars, stars, stoop down,
Stars, turn from your courses,
Spill into my hands!
Stars, you are my kindred:
I am strong with a new loneliness
That no one understands.

Youth Insatiate

If I have wished for skies unscarred by storm,
Shrunk from the grievous bitterness of things,
The days' perplexities, the nights' unrest,
The cruel, fruitless beating with clipped wings

Against the windows of the Infinite,
And, weary with the conflict's puerile stress,
Cried out against it all, cried out for peace,
Even what peace the rotting dead possess,

May Life forgive me: I am stronger now,
The play bewilders, but I know my part;
And I have learned that Beauty is salt blood
Pain-wrung from the unconquerable heart.

Let there be laughter then, love's wine and bread,
The many mouths of passion, their joys, their grief;
These are but soil and seed—for what grave growths?
I plant and wait, (and pray the time be brief!)

Lean wisdom this, to pause and taste and pause
Like a scared virgin who must stop for breath.
Take the cup simply, drain it to the lees;
Then, smiling, fling the empty cup to Death.

DISILLUSIONMENT

The agonies of disillusionment are the
growing-pains of Truth

Now I am done with ineffectual dreams,
Kindly play-toys of the unsure years,
And unencumbered, proud and free and light,
With even pulses and a lifting heart,
I mount the future's twisting stairs.

A week ago I thought that I must die,
Or hang forever, bitter as frost-killed fruit,
Scarred and broken from the Tree of Life—
Because I suddenly came into my sight

And men walked as trees; and dreams went mute.
'T is no small thing, to lose a dear, sure world,
To stumble, desolate, through hideous space,
Down unfamiliar and unfriendly roads
That bruise your feet. And then to suddenly feel
A great light newly shining in your face.

THE HOLE IN MY CURTAIN

It is because of the hole in my curtain.

I have stared through the torn space
Into Life's tortured face
As she leaned low and treadled her loom,
Watching, watching for the inevitable doom.
And I have seen the haggard shadows flit
Over the tapestries she wove, bit by bit,
Feverishly, her lips shrieking gay lies;
And always the tired song in her endless eyes.
I have watched the Form with his weary cynical face,
His pale smile, his definite, measured pace,
Gliding forward and gliding back like a thing condemned from end
    to end.
And calmly slitting Life's woven cloths

And they have wondered that I should laugh!
Marvelled at the potent wines I quaff.
Marvelled that I should dance on their God's dried flesh,
Shape a lute from a bone of His; weave a mesh
Of mirthless melody; that I should find Sin fair,
Circle her body and sleep in her odorous hair.
They have marveled that I should mock the day,
Throw my veil over the sun and smile at Fate's old play;
Lead my soul down the ribald, flowered path.
They have marveled. . . they have wondered
that I should laugh.
    in my curtain.
I have looked too long through the hole

Despair

I can laugh now.
Have you not heard my laughter?
It leads the winds:
They come tumbling and bubbling after.

I have learned to laugh.
I have learned to laugh with my spirit
And with my soul.
Listen. Do you not hear it?

I shall quench the world.
I shall sear the stars with my laughter;
Shrivel the moon and the sun
And make new ones after.

For life's skeleton
I shall make flesh from desires;
Then of my mounting laughter
Build it a temple with mocking spires.

I shall laugh to heaven.
I shall laugh below hell and above.
I shall laugh forever.
It was laughter God died of.

DECLARATION

I am a seed in the dust,
A live root bedded in night,
And I am filled with a lust
For something the worms call light.

From what seed-pod I was blown
Matters little to me,
Why and by whom I was sown
Or what the reaping may be.

I only wait for my hour
When I shall be done with night,
When I shall thrill into flower
And drink till I die of light.

THE POET

We are given pain to balance every joy,
We tragic-eyed divinities in dust.
Many the hearts life bleeds with little wounds,
The souls bewildered between God and lust.

We know the way of pity and pity's pain;
We know the unlit, endless street called Doubt;
And few but walk a black way at the end,
The piteous, hope-lit candles dead, burned out.

Yet these are mortal wounds of mortal thorns:
What of the few who suffer deadlier scars?
They are worse wounded than any in the world
Who bruise their lifted heads against the stars.

INNER CHAMBER

LOVE'S ACOLYTE

Many have loved you with lips and fingers
And lain with you till the moon went out;
Many have brought you lover's gifts;
And some have left their dreams on your doorstep.

But I who am youth among your lovers
Come like an acolyte to worship,
My thirsting blood restrained by reverence,
My heart a wordless prayer.

The candles of desire are lighted,
I bow my head, afraid before you,
A mendicant who craves your bounty
Ashamed of what small gifts he brings.

From the Top of the World

Come to me at the top of the world,
O Mine, before the years spill
Our rare love into Time's cup
And give our will to Time's will.

My wide basin is full of starlight,
My moon is lighted with new fire,
I have lit every sun in the firmament
With the hurting flame of my desire.

The worms there in the valley
Die—to forget death!
But here at the top of the world
I laugh under my breath.

There is pain here, and tears,
Bitter, terrible tears;
But the joys have warm mouths, and madness
Dances downwards with the years.

Come to me at the top of the world,
O Mine. The valley is deep,
The valley is full of the dying,
And with those that sleep.

But here wonderful winds blow
And the pines sing *one song*.
Come to me at the top of the world,
Come soon. I have waited too long.

Episode

I have robbed the garrulous streets,
Thieved a fair girl from their blight,
I have stolen her for a sacrifice
That I shall make to this mysteried night.

I have brought her, laughing,
To my quietly sinister garden.
For what will be done there
I ask no man's pardon.

I brush the rouge from her cheeks,
Clean the black kohl from the rims
Of her eyes; loose her hair;
Uncover the glimmering, shy limbs.

I break wild roses, scatter them over her.
The thorns between us sting like love's pain.
Her flesh, bitter and salt to my tongue,
I taste with endless kisses and taste again.

At dawn I leave her
Asleep in my wakening garden.
(For what was done there
I ask no man's pardon.)

EXPERIENCE

Now you are gone I kiss your dented pillow
And wonder if it hungers like my breast
For the dear head we both have held in rest.

I said once: Love alone cannot assuage
My thirst, my hunger, love has no reply
For that wild questioning, for this fierce cry.

I said: there is no kiss can feed me now.
Perhaps love is life's flower: I seek the root.
Yea, I have loved and love is dead sea fruit.

Yet I lie here and kiss your dented pillow,
A trembling girl who loves you overmuch—
A harp in anguish for the player's touch.

THIS IS NOT LOVE

This is not love: we cannot call it love.
Love would make me aware of infinite things,
Drive me down the spirit's vast abyss
And through the narrow fastnesses of pain.
This is not love. Yet it holds loveliness
Beyond mere pleasure. Peace and passion both
Grow from the kiss with which I paint drab hours.
It is not love: love is for the gods
And our more godlike moments. Yet when stars
Withhold their splendour, why should we not light
Candles to warm with kindly mortal flames
The all-enfolding, cold, immortal night?

A HAPPY SONG

Heaped sweets and a treasure
For a new sin to play with,
To pass a night and day with—
Heaped sweets for a pleasure.

Who and who will win them?
Who will carry virtue's pall?
Of what use are sins at all
If someone does not sin them?

Who will take the treasure?
Run and run on light-winged feet;
Who will buy my sweetest sweet
With a new found pleasure?

As Usual

You say you will not think of me:
You shut me out and count your beads,
The chaplet of your rules and doubts,
But lovers never think of creeds.

You'll fill your mind with serious things:
You'll think of God or Infinity,
Of a lover whose last charm is gone,
Of anything in the world but me.

Yet every thought will lead you back,
Infinity grow far and dim,
And God, with His sense of irony,
Will never let you think of Him.

THE ARTIST

Let us leave off loving, Madonna:
You have kissed me grey
And still I have no peace.
We thought we could make the night
A tapestry of passion.
Dear Love! What a vain caprice.

Where's the immortal design
We thought we had splashed on the indigo cloth?
And where is the cloth?
Dawn is forever the cynic.
He shows us love is the flame,
Our flesh the eternal moth.

Madonna. . . loose me and rise.
We are brief as apple-blossom
And I am heart-weary with thought of the end.
Creation is all.
The hours are thieves, Time a beggar,
And we have little to spend.

I ache for the brush in my hand.
The thrall of the compliant pigment
Governs my blood.
I will paint you, Madonna,
The afterlove glow in your face;

I would deify you if I could
With enchantments of color,
Bind you with fetters of terrible beauty
Fast to my canvas forever,
Give you the eternality God has denied you,
Bind you to life with art's sacred chains
That death cannot sever.

Love has betrayed us enough with its treacherous wonder:
Let us go now while we ache with the magic
Or what is the gain?
Art is our one immortality,
All we may win from the gods
In exchange for our labor and pain.

Sudden Friendship

Yesterday we walked apart,
Separate and cold and mortal.
Now the mystic kiss has joined us,
Now we stand inside the portal

That permits of no returning,
And my heart is strangely burning.

I know not what the word may be,
Or what the charm, or what the token,
That has filled us with this glory.
But never let the charm be broken.

Let it stay a mystery
For all time to be.

Yesterday, with lighter joys,
We wantoned at the outer portal.
Now, with love's old alchemy,
We have made ourselves immortal.

Love Song

My love, you destroy me, you rend,
    You tear me apart.
You are a wild swan I have caught
    And housed in my heart.

My sister, my love, I am shattered,
    Broken, dismayed.
The live wings, the wild wings are beating,
    They make me afraid.

Fold your wings, brood like a dove,
    Be a dove I can cherish
More calmly, my dear, my tempestuous love,
    Or I perish.

Late Autumn Afternoon

Grey, fingered with flickering threads of light;
Silence broken by restless quavers of music.
Greyness, music,
A playing thought of slumber.
And on my lips faintly disturbing fingers,
And at my heart love's hand like a child's hand
Stirring me half awake.

Philosophy

Since we must soon be fed
As honey and new bread
To ever-hungiy Death:
O, love me very sweet
And kiss me very long
And let us use our breath
For song.
Nothing else endures
Overlong.

You Are Not She

You are not she I loved. You cannot be
    My wild, white dove,
My tempest-driven dove that I gave house,
    You cannot be my Love.

She died. I used to hold her all night long;
    Come awake
At dawn beside her. Try to ease with loving
    A thirst too deep to slake.

O, it was pain to keep her shut against me.
    Honey and bitterness
To taste her with sharp kisses and hold her after
    In brief duress.

You cold woman, you stranger with her ways,
    Smiling cruelly,
You tear my heart as never her wild wings' beating
    Wounded me.

Love Sleep

Watch my Love in sleep:
Is she not beautiful
As a young flower at night
Weary and glad with dew?

Pale curved body
That I have kissed too much,
Warm with slumber's flush;
Breasts like mounded snow,
Too small for children's mouths;
Lips a red spring bud
My love will bring to bloom.

How restlessly she moves!
She, no more than a child,
Stirs like a woman troubled
With guilt of secret sins.

Twin furtive tears
Glide from the shadows,
Her eyes' shadowed blue.
Her dreaming must be sad.

What grief to watching love
That it is impotent,
For all its reckless strength,
When the sleep gates close.

When Love Becomes a Stranger

When Love becomes a stranger
In the temple he has built
Of remembered nights and days,
When he sighs and turns away
From the altar in the temple
With unreturning feet,
When the candles flicker out
And the magical-sweet incense
Vanishes. . .
Do you think there is grief born
In any god's heart?

Of a Certain Friendship

Odd how you entered my house quietly,
Quietly left again.
While you stayed you ate at my table,
Slept in my bed.
There was much sweetness,
Yet little was done, little said.
After you left there was pain,
Now there is no more pain.

But the door of a certain room in my house
Will be always shut.
Your fork, your plate, the glass you drank from,
The music you played,
Are in that room
With the pillow where last your head was laid.
And there is one place in my garden
Where it's best that I set no foot.

Constancy

You're jealous if I kiss this girl and that.
You think I should be constant to one mouth.
Little you know of my too quenchless drouth.
My sister, I keep faith with love, not lovers.

Life laid a flaming finger on my heart,
Gave me an electric golden thread,
Pointed to a pile of beads and said:
Link me one more perfect than the rest.

Love's the thread, my sister, you a bead,
An ivory one, you are so delicate.
These first burned ash-grey—far too passionate.
Farther on the colors mount and sing.

When the last bead's painted with the last design
And slipped upon the thread, I'll tie it so,
Then smiling quietly, I'll turn and go
While vain Life boasts her latest ornament.

Mnasidika

I shall not harm you at all nor ask you for anything,
You need have no fear;
I am only very tired and would like to rest awhile
With my head here
And play with the long strands of your loosed hair,
Or touch your skin,
Feel your cool breath on my eyes, watch it stir
Those rising hills where your breasts begin;
And listen to your voice whispering tender words
Until, perhaps, I fall asleep;
Or feel you kiss my forehead to comfort me a little
If I should weep.
That is all, just to lie so beside you
Till dawn's lamp is lit.
You need not fear me. I have given too much of love
Ever to ask for it.

The Friend Departs

'Tis not alone that you have gone from me:
All the hungry, fragile roots of hope
Are blasted by a Thing I cannot name;
And I am desolate remembering

The rare kiss, the intimate silent climbing
From passion to a breathless comprehension.
Even my peace of heart, born of long pain,
Dies, drowned in a turbulence of passion.

Life today is like a glass reflecting
Nothing more than my own grieving eyes,
Or like a goblet that I sit and stare at,
Empty of all but stains of last night's wine.

I, Lover

I shall never have any fear of love,
Not of its depth nor its uttermost height,
Its exquisite pain and its terrible delight.
I shall never have any fear of love.

I shall never hesitate to go down
Into the fastness of its abyss
Nor shrink from the cruelty of its awful kiss.
I shall never have any fear of love.

Never shall I dread love's strength
Nor any pain it might give.
Through all the years I may live
I shall never have any fear of love.

I shall never draw back from love
Through fear of its vast pain
But build joy of it and count it again.
I shall never have any fear of love.

I shall never tremble nor flinch
From love's moulding touch:
I have loved too terribly and too much
Ever to have any fear of love.

Relinquishment

Go her way, her quiet, quiet way,
Her way is best for one so wistful-tired.
My three-months' lover, go with your world-sick heart,
Your love-bruised flesh. I am no sanctuary.

This hot mouth, these ardent, out-reaching arms,
This hollow between my breasts, these hungry limbs,
They are a cradle, a cradle of living flame;
No haven for you, saddening after peace.

I am not certain, no, nor soothing-safe.
Mine is the shifting, perilous way of life.
Pitiless, ever-changing, hazardous,
My love insatiate and mutable.

Go her way, her quiet, well-path'd way,
Sit by her hearth-fire; let her keep you safe.
Mine the unharbored heart, the uncharted passions;
Mine, at the end a more than common peace.

IN PASSING

The Face in the Rain

O form! O face!
Elfin face in the crowd!
Form, face, white throat,
Pale throat wound with a scarf
Poppy red,
Blood-like, red,
Pale throat wound with a poppy scarf
Gleaming out of the crowd.
    Background of grey,
    A rain-wet street;
    Shuffling; shambling
    Beating feet,
    Past the corner where four ways meet.
O face, O throat!
Crimson and white
Splashed on grey:
I have thought of nothing else all day.
    Misted streets,
    A scarf-wound throat,
    Fay-like face
    That seemed to float
    Through the crowd
    Like a wisp of song:
    I have thought of them all day long.

GREY SKIES

I like grey skies,
At least they tell the truth;
Grey skies,
Reflective skies
That do not laugh at all
Nor weep vain tears.
Unpromising,
Unhoping,
Cold.

Grey skies,
No fear in them
Nor any joy,
No tragedy,
All grey.
I like grey skies,
Unweeping, smileless skies.
They do not lie.

CHANT OF SPRING

Like an unhappy woman Earth frees herself from the arms of Winter,
Surely Winter, her indifferent Lord,
Whose touch is death to her passionate body,
And, weeping, yields to Spring, the wooing maiden,
The slim girl who kisses her with awakening kisses,
Burning her lips and eyelids with flaming mouth loosed upon them,
Renewing her body with wildness of young caresses,
Holding her close while the reckless hours dance to death.

Wan passion flowers growing in hidden places,
Memories,
Kisses given by the slim maiden.
Wan passion flowers,
All that is left to Earth of her maddest lover.

Dawn

Dawn opens like a great gold flower,
Petal by monstrous petal,
Quivering minute by minute,
Hour by hour.
Stretches great live leaves over hundreds of hills,
Scatters flakes of pollen dust into a few valleys,
Drops a loose petal down where a slender waterfall spills.

Morning opens like a gold flower,
Stirs and quivers singingly at the feet of day;
Shoots transparent light into a moving mist
That twists spirally
Like a butterfly at play.

In the heart of the mist, morning opens, a gold flower,
Superbly, like a dawning passion.
Can night be the consummation
Of this expectant white hour?

Poppy Song

Love in a garden of poppies
Playing at living life,
Love with smiles in her speech,
Love dancing at dawn
In a garden of flushed pink poppies.

Love, unsmiling now,
At noon in the garden of poppies,
With a laugh under her eyelids,
Fear deep in her eyes,
And tangled with her hair,
Sighs and a struggling joy.

Love, with a dim, strained face,
At night in the garden of poppies,
Her lips crushing the bloom
From the fairest flower there.
Love drunk with the wine
She has drawn from the poppy's heart:
Love with death at her breasts.

Love at the end of night
Shaded by drooping poppies;
Love with scattered hair
And strange stains on her lips.
Love with death at her breasts.

To a Young Dancing Girl

Golden-eyed girl, do you see what I see?
Do you see behind the veil that Life laughs through?
Golden-eyed girl, I would like to laugh with you.
But my veil is torn, and I see things pass
Like shadows in the depths of a crystal glass.

Golden-eyed girl, you are young as springtime,
Your great eyes are dreamful, your rare lips sweet.

Shadows matter little to youth with dancing feet
All of Life's skeletons wear gay dresses
And youth is deceived by even Death's caresses.

Golden-eyed girl, you have years to dance and wonder
Before your Life's curtain will wear into holes
And let you see the hopelessness hidden in souls.
You have many moons of laughter, many years to go
Before you'll learn how heavy dancing feet can grow.

CHANCE

Strange that a single white iris
Given carelessly one slumbering spring midnight
Should be the first of love,
Yet life is written so.

If it had been a rose
I might have smiled and pinned it to my dress:
We should have said Good Night indifferently
And never met again.
But the white iris!
It looked so infinitely pure
In the thin green moonlight.
A thousand little purple things
That had trembled about me through the young years
Floated into a shape I seem always to have known
That I suddenly called Love!

The faint touch of your long fingers on mine wakened me.
I saw that your tumbled hair was bright with flame,

That your eyes were sapphire souls with hungry stars in them,
And your lips were too near not to be kissed.

Life crouches at the knees of Chance
And takes what falls to her.

LONELINESS

This loneliness encaged in me
That has no curious heart for life,
No ribald blood, no treacherous flesh
Nor golden wickedness of song,
This loneliness that prays in me,
Is it not somewhat like a nun?
See the clasped hands, the secret eyes,
The lips pressed close for fear of love!
What if I make her drunk one day
With wine or some unholy need
Then leave the cell door open wide—
Think you she might be tempted out?

Before Sleep

There is an autumn sadness upon me,
A sadness of bared trees,
And mist and delicate death of flowers.
There is an autumn sadness upon me,

A falling of leaves in my soul.
There is an autumn sadness upon me,
A dreamfulness in my heart,
And a wistful sense of longing.
There is faint moaning music
Like cries of departing birds.

There are trembling hands on my eyelids,
A dim foreknowledge of tears
And dreams, patterning ultimate slumber.
There is an autumn sadness upon me,
A falling of leaves in my soul.

A Thought

There are more songs in the far corners of my soul
Than I shall ever be able to sing.
I shall go away long before they are all expressed
And they will wait for another life, for more suffering,
To give them birth; another life and many more tears
And love, to make them open their eyes to the light.
It will take many lives to express all the songs
I hear singing to themselves day and night.

EPILOGUE

Epilogue

Why are you laughing, Poet?
I much prefer your sighs.
I myself have just read one of your songs
And tears are biting my eyes.

And why should I not laugh?
I cleaned my heart of its dust,
Swept my spirit clear of its cobwebs,
Gathered them up and thrust
Them from me. And then
Men passing, found the whole,
Called them songs and sang them and exulted.
They thought they had found my soul.

A Note About the Author

Elsa Gidlow (1898–1986) was a Canadian American poet, journalist, and philosopher. Born in Yorkshire, England, Gidlow moved with her family to Canada in 1905, settling in Montreal. At seventeen, she began pursuing amateur journalism full time, working with Roswell George Mills to publish *Les Mouche fantastique*, a pioneering magazine that was the first in North America dedicated to gay and lesbian content. Gidlow left for New York at 21, finding work as a poetry editor of *Pearson's* and befriending influential poet Kenneth Rexroth, whom she would follow to San Francisco in 1926. A lesbian and anarchist, Gidlow was involved in some of California's most influential radical political and artistic circles, befriending Dizzy Gillespie, Louis Armstrong, Robert Duncan, Ram Dass, Allen Ginsberg, and Maya Angelou throughout her life. At her ranch Druid Heights, purchased in 1954 and shared with her partner Isabel Grenfell Quallo and carpenter Roger Somers, she established a bohemian community that was home to such figures as Alan Watts, Gary Snyder, and Catherine MacKinnon. Persecuted by the United States government's House Un-American Activities Committee for her beliefs, Gidlow was a tireless artist and activist whose autobiographical works, philosophical texts on lesbianism, and poetry collections—including her debut *On a Grey Thread* (1923)—remain essential, groundbreaking works of queer literature.

A Note from the Publisher

Spanning many genres, from non-fiction essays to literature classics to children's books and lyric poetry, Mint Edition books showcase the master works of our time in a modern new package. The text is freshly typeset, is clean and easy to read, and features a new note about the author in each volume. Many books also include exclusive new introductory material. Every book boasts a striking new cover, which makes it as appropriate for collecting as it is for gift giving. Mint Edition books are only printed when a reader orders them, so natural resources are not wasted. We're proud that our books are never manufactured in excess and exist only in the exact quantity they need to be read and enjoyed. To learn more and view our library, go to minteditionbooks.com

bookfinity & MINT EDITIONS

Enjoy more of your favorite classics with Bookfinity,
a new search and discovery experience for readers.
With Bookfinity, you can discover more vintage
literature for your collection, find your Reader Type,
track books you've read or want to read,
and add reviews to your favorite books.
Visit www.bookfinity.com, and click on
Take the Quiz to get started.

Don't forget to follow us
@bookfinityofficial and @mint_editions

CPSIA information can be obtained
at www.ICGtesting.com
Printed in the USA
FSHW022321270521
81885FS